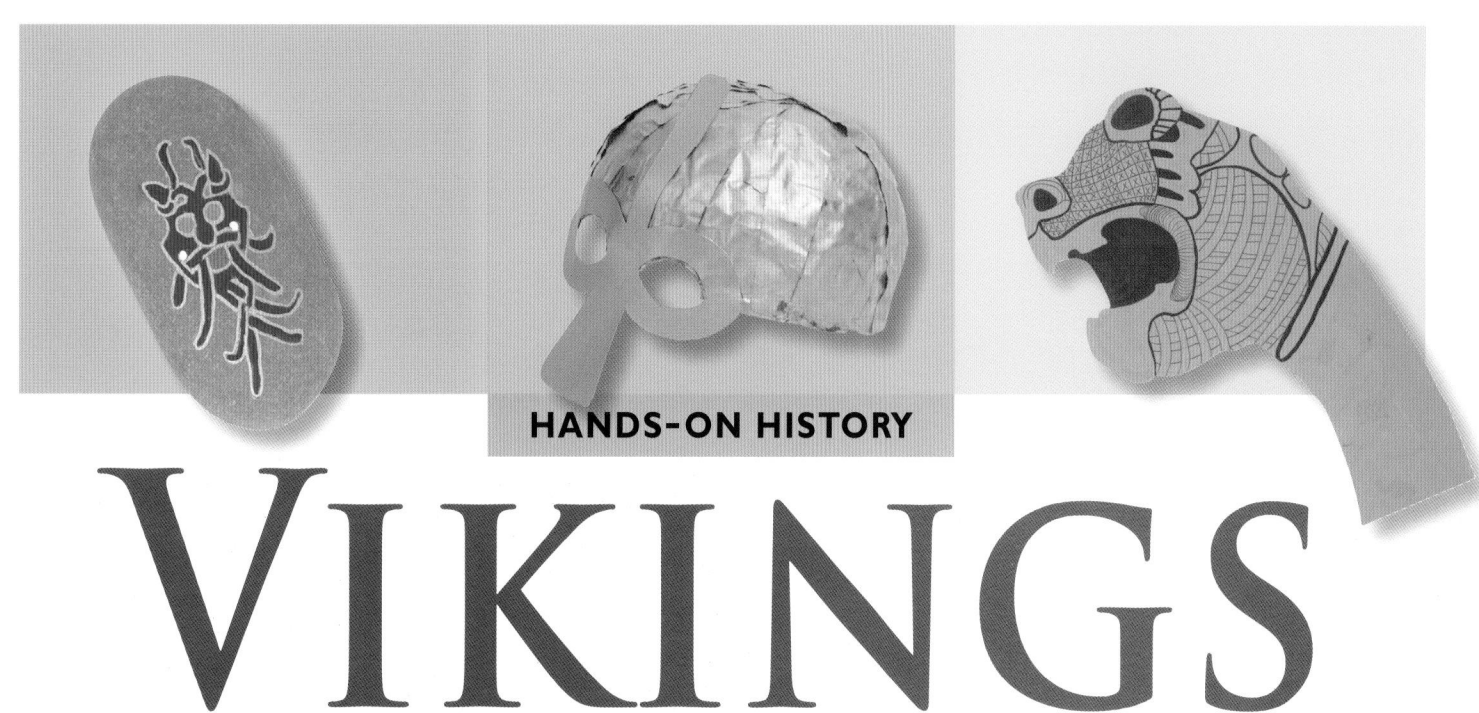

HANDS-ON HISTORY

VIKINGS

DRESS, EAT, WRITE AND PLAY JUST LIKE THE VIKINGS

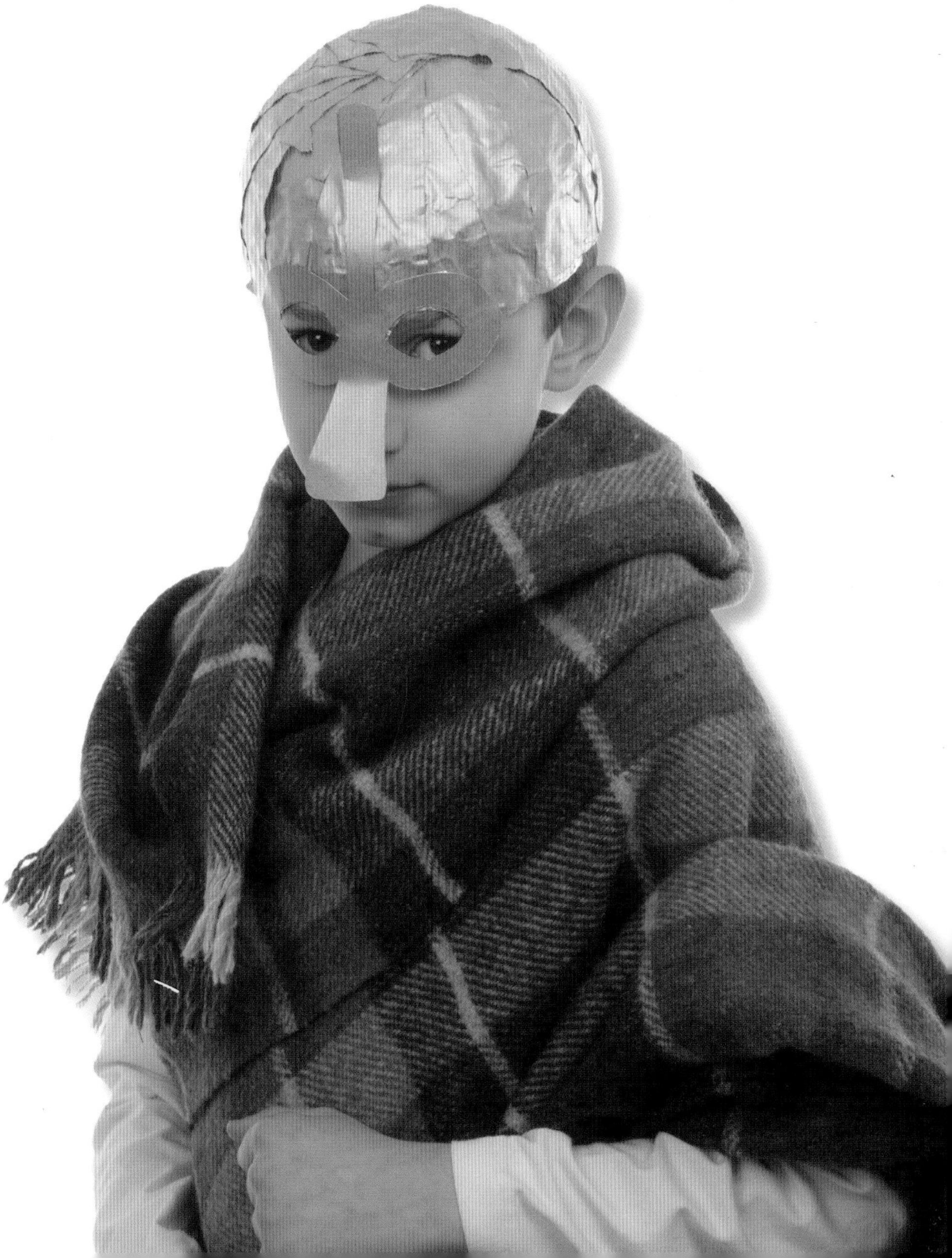

FIONA MACDONALD

QED Publishing

Written by Fiona Macdonald
Editor Felicity Fitchard
Designer Liz Wiffen
Projects made by Veronica Erard

Publisher Steve Evans
Creative Director Zeta Davies
Senior Editor Hannah Ray

Printed and bound in China

Picture credits

Key: t = top, b = bottom, c = centre, l = left, r = right,
fc = front cover

akg-images: p6 tr Jürgen Sorges.

The Art Archive: p4 br Prehistoric Museum Moesgard
Høberg Denmark/Dagli Orti; p8 tl, p20 tl Musée de la
Tapisserie Bayeux/Dagli Orti.

Corbis: p28 tl: Charles & Josette Lenars.

Dorling Kindersley: p12 tr; p14 tr Alan Keohane; p18
bl Geoff Dann; p28 cb Peter Anderson/Danish National
Museum.

TopFoto: p26 tr.

Werner Forman Archive: FC, p16 tl Universitetets
Oldsaksamling, Oslo; p4 tl, p8 br, p14 bl Statens
Historiska Museum, Stockholm; p6 bl National Museum,
Denmark; p10 tl Bergen Maritime Museum; p10 bl Viking
Ship Museum, Bygdoy; p16 bl University of National
Antiquities, Uppsala, Sweden; p18 tr, p24 t&b, p26 bl
National Museum, Copenhagen.

Paul Windett courtesy of **Ydalir Vikings**: p12 bl, p20 bl,
p22 t&b. (www.ydlair.co.uk)

Words in **bold** are explained
in the glossary on page 30.

Website information is correct at the time of
going to press. However, the publisher cannot
accept liability for any information or links
found on third-party websites.

Before undertaking an activity which involves
eating or the preparation of food, parents
and/or teachers should ensure that none of
the children in their care are allergic to any
of the ingredients. In a classroom situation,
prior written permission from parents may
be required.

CONTENTS

WHO WERE THE VIKINGS?

The Vikings came from Norway, Denmark and Sweden. They attacked the coasts of northern Europe from around 800 to 1100 CE, bringing terror to peaceful places. They stole money, destroyed houses and churches, and captured people to sell as slaves. But the Vikings were not just bloodthirsty bandits. They were tough sailors, clever **merchants**, skilful craftworkers and bold explorers. They were also hard-working **settlers**, who built new farms, villages, forts and towns.

▲ Small, silver head showing a Viking warrior, found in Aska, Sweden. No one knows who he was or where he fought and died.

The Viking homelands in northern Europe were surrounded by stormy seas to the east, west and south, and by Arctic ice to the north. ▶

ICELAND NORWAY
GREENLAND SWEDEN
ATLANTIC OCEAN
DENMARK RUSSIA
NEWFOUNDLAND
Normandy

DID YOU KNOW?

THESE ARE ALL VIKING WORDS: BOTH, DRAG, EGG, FALL, GALE, KNIFE, SCORE, SCOLD, SHIP, SLING, SLUG, SMILE, WANT, WHIRL, WHISTLE, WINDOW AND WING.

JARLS AND THINGS

The first Viking lands were ruled by **jarls** (nobles). Over time, as Viking society grew larger, the most successful jarls became kings. Viking villagers held public meetings, called 'Things', once a year to decide how their communities should be run.

Monster face with horns and a long beard carved on a stone in Viking Denmark. ▶

VIKING WANDERERS

Viking kings, jarls and ordinary people travelled vast distances to trade and find new land. Wherever they settled, they brought their own language, beliefs, traditions and skills. Even today, many places in Europe have Viking names, and north European languages contain Viking words.

4

PAINT A VIKING STONE

The Vikings painted stones to record their history and stories of gods and monsters. Make your own Viking stone in five easy steps.

YOU WILL NEED:
SMOOTH STONE OR PEBBLE • WASHING-UP BOWL • WASHING-UP LIQUID • CHALK OR WHITE PENCIL • ACRYLIC PAINTS • BRUSHES • GOLD METALLIC PEN • ACRYLIC VARNISH OR PVA MIXTURE (3 PARTS PVA, ONE PART WATER)

1 Find a smooth stone or pebble in the garden or park. Wash it in soapy water, rinse and leave to dry.

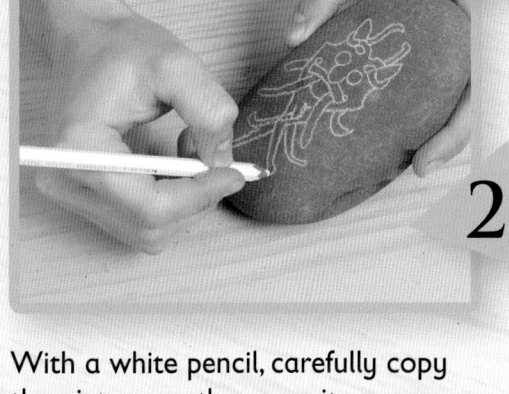

2 With a white pencil, carefully copy the picture on the opposite page onto your stone.

3 Paint the face blue, except for the eyes and mouth. Paint the mouth red and add a white dot on each side.

4 Paint the eyes light blue. Once all the paint is dry, use a gold metallic pen to go over your lines.

5 Use a clean brush to add a coat of PVA mixture as varnish. Leave to dry, then add another coat.

Use your stone as a paperweight or display it on a shelf. ▶

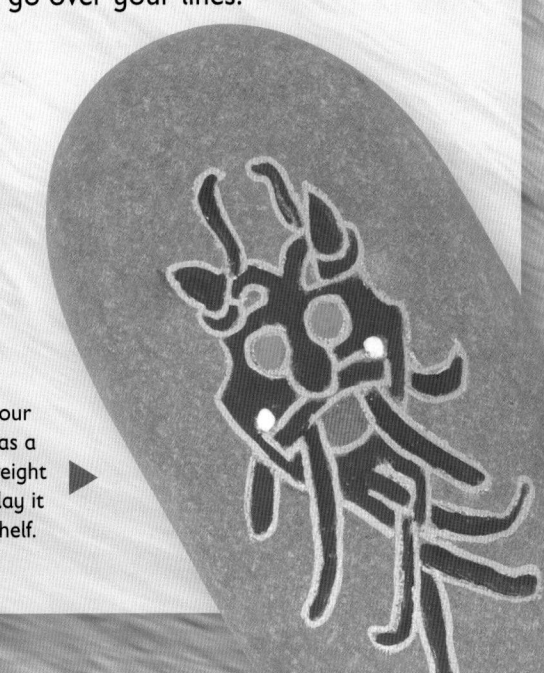

5

SURVIVAL SKILLS

The Vikings lived in the north of Europe, where the winters were long and snowy, and the summers were short. Families survived by growing oats and barley, and raising sheep, goats and cattle. They planted apple and plum trees, and created gardens to grow onions, peas and cabbages. In the summer, they cut grass and dried it to make hay for their animals to eat later in the year.

▲

Viking homes were made of wood, stone or turf (slabs of earth with growing grass). Roofs were also made of turf, or they were thatched (covered with dried straw). This is a reconstruction of a Viking home, with modern windows!

DID YOU KNOW?

THE VIKINGS BURNED WHALE-OIL IN LAMPS, TO LIGHT THEIR HOMES, AND RUBBED BLUBBER (FAT) FROM SEALS INTO THEIR SHOES AND LEATHER WAISTCOATS TO MAKE THEM WATERPROOF.

FORAGING FOR FOOD

Most Viking families lived close to the sea. They went fishing and caught large sea-creatures, such as whales and seals. They hunted wild birds to eat, and wild animals, such as wolves, foxes and reindeer, for their skins and furs. They gathered shellfish, birds' eggs, wild mushrooms, nuts and berries. In the winter, when there were fewer animals to kill and nothing grew, Vikings went hungry and sometimes starved.

HOME AND HEARTH

A typical Viking house had thick walls to keep out the cold, and one big room where the family lived and slept. In the middle of the room, a fire was kept burning all the time, for warmth and for cooking. Viking homes were often smoky inside. Many houses had storerooms and work-rooms close by, together with barns for animals, called byres (say buy-ers).

▲

Viking homes did not have much furniture apart from wooden tables, stools or benches, and storage chests. Women kept the keys to the chests.

Make a Viking Chest

Transform a shoe box into a chest for storing your treasures. Opening a chest without permission was a serious crime in Viking times.

YOU WILL NEED:
PAIR OF COMPASSES • PENCIL
SHOE BOX • RULER • A1 SHEET
OF THIN CARD • SCISSORS •
GLUE • BROWN PAINT •
BRUSH • GOLD CARD •
BLACK MARKER PEN

1 Using a pair of compasses and a ruler, draw two semicircles that are the same width as your shoe box.

2 Extend the compass and around each semicircle, draw a slightly larger one. Cut out, around the larger semi-circles.

3 Cut in tabs. Draw a rectangle that's the same length as your shoe box and two and a half times its width.

4 Cut out the rectangle. Now glue a semicircle to each long edge of the the rectangle, a few tabs at a time.

5 Paint the shoe box and new lid. Add strips of gold card. Glue the overlap on the lid to the back of the shoe box.

Stick on a small square of gold card and draw on a key hole. Decorate the strips with a black marker pen.

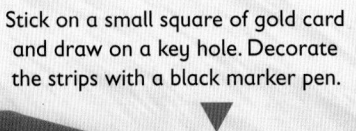

7

RAIDERS FROM THE NORTH

This detail from the **Bayeux Tapestry** shows **Norman** warriors sailing their warships to invade England.

Vikings used the threat of raids to demand money from other nations. These payments were called 'Danegeld' (say dane-geld). If foreign kings refused to pay, Viking raiders attacked their lands. Each Viking king or jarl recruited local farmers to fight for him in his own private army called a lid (say lith). He expected them to be fiercely loyal to him, and to each other. In return, he rewarded them with treasures, and protected them from rival armies.

GOING BERSERK
Viking armies had troops of special wild warriors, called berserkers (say bear-ser-kerrs). They wore clothes made from bearskin, and believed the skins gave them magic powers. Before fighting, they worked themselves into a fury, howling and chewing their shields.

This helmet was designed to give extra protection to the wearer's eyes and nose. The crest on top helped guard his brain.

COURAGE AND CONVICTION
The Vikings admired strength and courage in both men and women. While men were away, Viking women ran the farms and defended family land from attackers. Many Viking raiders never came back — they were killed fighting or lost at sea. Viking people were expected to face death bravely. Viking poets said, 'Cattle die, families die, we ourselves must die.'

WEAR A JARL'S HELMET

Jarls wore strong metal helmets to protect their heads and scare their enemies. No one will recognize you behind this nose guard!

1 Blow up a balloon. Dip torn-up strips of newspaper into PVA mixture. Stick them to the top half of the balloon.

2 Build up several layers of papier-mâché strips. Leave to dry. (This may take several hours.)

3 Pop the balloon and remove it. Use scissors to trim the jagged edges straight, all the way round.

4 Draw the eye and nose piece onto card. Ask an adult to cut it out with a craft knife.

5 Glue the eye and nose piece to the papier-mâché helmet. When the glue is dry, paint the helmet gold.

If you want your helmet to shine, ask an adult to spray-paint it for you. Make sure they do it outside! ▶

9

DRAGON SHIPS

This 21.5m-long wooden ship has a snake-shaped **prow**. It was made in Norway over 1000 years ago.

Vikings lived in wild, harsh places. There were few roads or bridges, so it was difficult to travel overland. It was quicker and easier for Vikings to travel by boat – along rivers, around the coast or across the ocean. They made small, light boats for short coastal journeys and big boats called knarr (say naarr) with wide, deep **hulls** for longer voyages. Viking traders used knarr to carry goods overseas to sell. For raiding, the Vikings built fast, sleek warships. The biggest and best were called dragon ships, or drakkar (say drack-arr).

YOU WILL NEED:
TRACING PAPER • PENCIL • RULER • A1 SHEET CARD • BLACK AND WHITE PAINT • BRUSHES • CRAFT KNIFE

MAKE A DRAGON HEAD

Dragons appear in a lot of Viking art because they were fierce, wild and mysterious – just like famous Viking heroes.

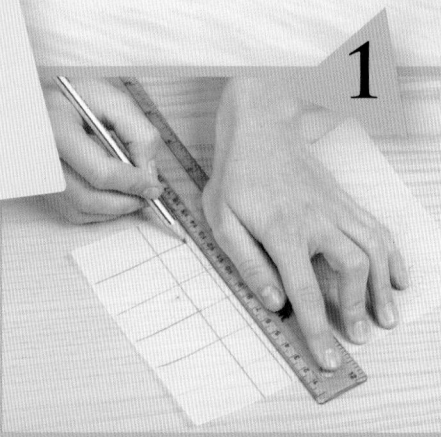

1

Draw a grid of 2cm squares onto tracing paper. Put the grid over the dragon on the left. Draw round it.

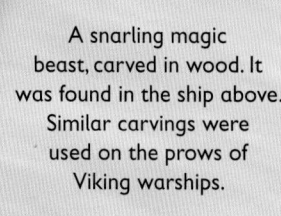

A snarling magic beast, carved in wood. It was found in the ship above. Similar carvings were used on the prows of Viking warships.

3

Copy the contents of each square on the tracing paper grid into the matching square on the big grid.

BUILDING SHIPS

The largest Viking drakkar so far discovered is 30 metres long and 3.7 metres wide. Whatever their size, all Viking ships were built from overlapping wooden planks. These were fastened to a heavy oak **keel** (the 'backbone') with strong iron nails. Tall pine-tree trunks were used for **masts**, and a steering oar was fitted at the **stern**.

MASTER SEAFARERS

It took around 120 men, two to each oar, to row a big, fast drakkar. Viking ships were designed with streamlined hulls to skim over the waves, rather than ploughing through them. This made them less likely to fill with water and sink. The Vikings were proud of their ships, and gave them splendid names, such as 'Long Serpent'.

DID YOU KNOW?
In winter, when rivers, lakes and bogs were frozen, Vikings travelled on sledges, skates and skis.

Prop your dragon head up behind your bed or next to your bedroom door.

2

On a card sheet, draw a large grid of 10 x 10cm squares. Both grids need the same number of squares.

4

Mix white and black paint to make grey. Paint your dragon head and leave it to dry completely.

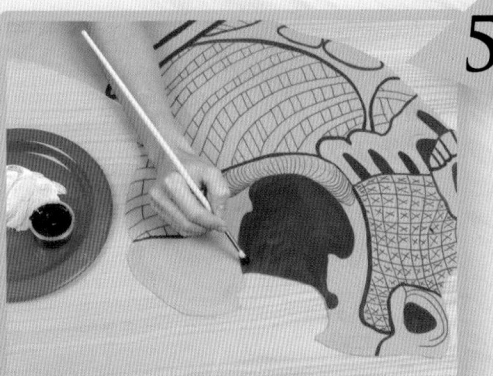

5

Ask an adult to cut out your dragon head. Draw on details, such as the eye. Go over with black paint.

11

WEAPONS AND ARMOUR

Viking battles were mostly fought on foot. Warriors leaped from their ships or lined up behind their leaders – then charged! Sometimes, they threw a single spear before attacking. They did this to show that they claimed all the men they were going to kill for the Viking war-god, Odin.

Viking warriors had to provide their own weapons and armour, or steal them on raids! The man on the left is wearing chain mail.

DID YOU KNOW?

KINGS HAD BLOOD-CURDLING NICKNAMES SUCH AS 'RUTHLESS', 'BLOODAXE', 'IRONSIDE', 'FLATNOSE' AND 'HAIRY-BREEKS' (WHICH MEANS HAIRY TROUSERS).

WEAPONS AT THE READY

Vikings fought using several different weapons, but their favourites were long, sharp swords and heavy battleaxes. They used these to hack, stab and bash their enemies at **close quarters**. Warriors also hurled spears and shot arrows from bows to attack enemies from a distance. Swords, axes, spear-tips and arrowheads were all crafted from iron. Bows and spear-shafts were made of wood. The best weapons were decorated with real gold and silver, and had names such as 'Stinger' and 'Leg Biter'.

Banners were carried on tall poles so that Viking warriors could see where their leaders were on the battlefield, and follow them.

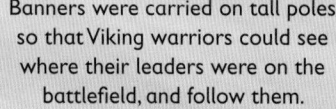

DRESSED TO FIGHT

For protection in battle, ordinary Vikings wore tough leather caps and **tunics**. Kings, chiefs and other top warriors had iron helmets and chain-mail armour made from hundreds of iron rings linked together. Warriors carried circular shields made of wood and leather strengthened with iron. These guarded a warrior's body, from his shoulders to his knees.

MAKE A BATTLE BANNER

Viking warriors carried banners high as they went into battle. Banners often had pictures of strong, fierce animals painted on them.

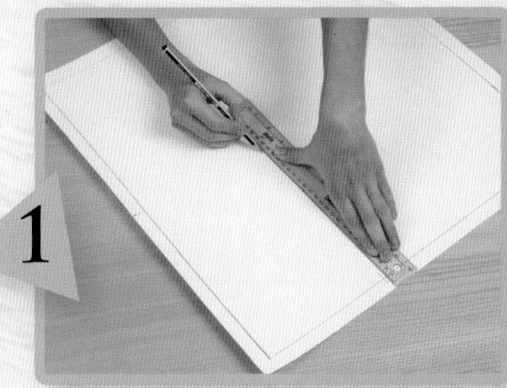

1

Draw a 58 x 44cm rectangle on card. Make a mark a third in from one long edge and halfway along.

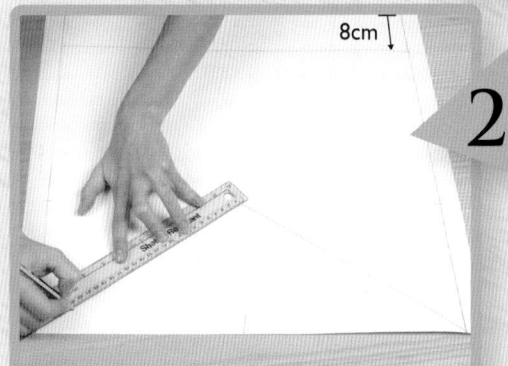

2

8cm

Join up the corners to the mark. Draw a vertical margin line 8cm in from the other long edge.

3

Draw eight equally spaced horizontal lines in the margin. Copy the boar from this page onto the banner.

4

Go over the boar, strips and edges in black felt-tip pen and paint the background blue.

5

Cut the banner out. Cut away every other strip down the margin. Fix the remaining strips around the dowel.

You could paint the back of your banner, too, so that it looks the same from both sides. ▶

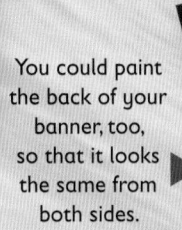

EXPLORERS AND SETTLERS

Settlers worked hard to build houses in new lands. They also built boats for fishing.

Daring Viking explorers sailed vast distances across unknown seas and oceans. They were searching for new goods to trade and new lands to farm. Some also hoped to find new kingdoms to rule, away from their rivals in the Viking homelands.

HEADING WEST
In 795 CE, Vikings from Norway headed west, to settle in Scotland and Ireland. Later, they reached Iceland (870 CE) and then Greenland (983 CE). From Greenland, they sailed across the Atlantic Ocean to Vinland (now Newfoundland, Canada), in around 1000 CE.

DID YOU KNOW?
EXPLORERS KNEW THEY WERE NEAR LAND WHEN THEY SAW SEAWEED, ICEBERGS, BIRDS – OR SMELT SHEEP!

OTHER ADVENTURES
Around 750 CE, Swedish Vikings headed east, to set up forts and camps in Russia. From 860 CE, Vikings from Denmark began to settle in north and east England. They ruled a kingdom there until 1042 CE. Some settlers were women. For example, Aud the Deep-Minded was the wife and daughter of chiefs. She led her family to settle in Iceland around 880 CE.

Ships carrying explorers and settlers had weather-vanes fitted to their masts or prows.

MAKE A WEATHER VANE

Vikings fitted weather vanes to their ships, to show which way the wind was blowing. Make a stunning weather vane from foil card.

YOU WILL NEED:
A4 TRACING PAPER • PENCIL • GOLD FOIL CARD • CRAFT KNIFE • CUTTING BOARD • FINE BLACK MARKER PEN

1

Copy the weather vane on page 14 onto tracing paper. Go over lightly first and then darken all your lines.

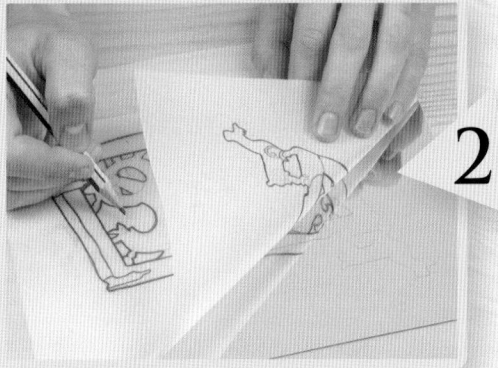

2

Transfer the tracing onto gold foil card. You'll have to press hard to make an impression.

3

Ask an adult to cut out your weather vane with a craft knife on a cutting board.

4

Use a fine black marker pen to add decoration around the edge and details to the horse.

You could attach your weather vane to a dowel rod with sticky tape. Alternatively, fix your weather vane to the window with adhesive putty. ▶

15

CRAFTS, MARKETS AND TOWNS

There were several large, rich trading towns in the Viking homelands. The most famous were Hedeby in Denmark, Birka in Sweden, York in England and Dublin in Ireland. These towns were planned, defended and owned by Viking kings. Highly skilled craftworkers lived and worked in towns, making fine iron weapons, gold and silver jewellery, delicate ivory combs, embroidered clothes and carved wooden furniture.

▲ Viking wood-carving showing a blacksmith (left) holding red-hot iron with tongs while he hammers it into shape. His helper (right) uses bellows to fan the fire that heats the iron.

YOU WILL NEED:
PAIR OF COMPASSES • 2 PLASTIC LIDS • STRING • SCISSORS • DRINKING STRAW

MAKE A MERCHANT'S SCALES

Traders carried a small set of scales and weights with them to work out the value of coins from different lands.

▲ Scales used by a travelling merchant. The merchant would have held them in his hand, put silver coins in one pan, and little weights in the other. When the top bar was level, he could tell how much the coins weighed.

1

With the point of a compass, make four evenly spaced holes around the edge of each lid.

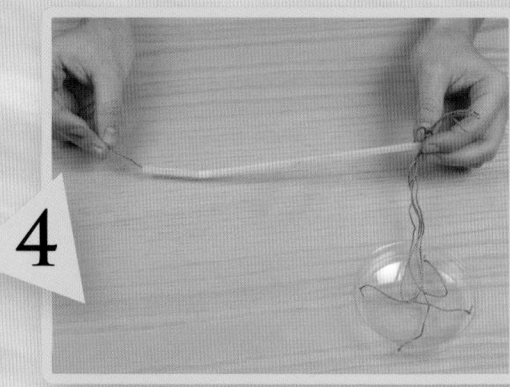

4

Cut a 25cm length of string. Tie the end to the knot above one lid. Then feed the string through the straw.

GOODS AND MERCHANTS

Travelling merchants visited Viking towns to sell luxuries from foreign lands. Rich Viking customers prized glass from Germany, wine from France and silk from Asia. Raiders also brought captives to towns, to sell as slaves. Viking slaves helped with ordinary tasks and some were taught craft skills. For example, they might spend all day, everyday, weaving wool.

THE LOCAL MARKET

At country markets, Viking farmers and their families **bartered** farm produce for other local goods, such as honey, wax, dried fish, wooden buckets, willow baskets, iron nails, amber beads and stout leather shoes. Coins were not widely used by ordinary Viking people. Sometimes hack-silver (silver scrap) was used for buying and selling, instead.

2

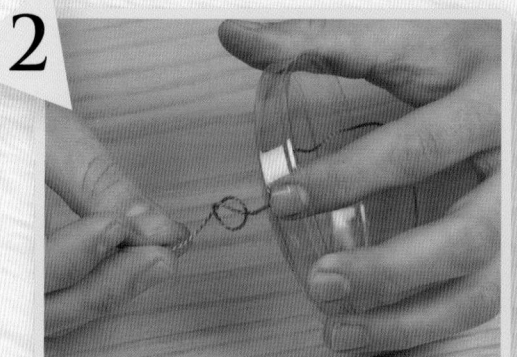

Cut eight 25cm lengths of string. Feed a length of string through each hole on both lids and knot.

3

On each lid, pull all four strings up to the same height and knot them together.

5

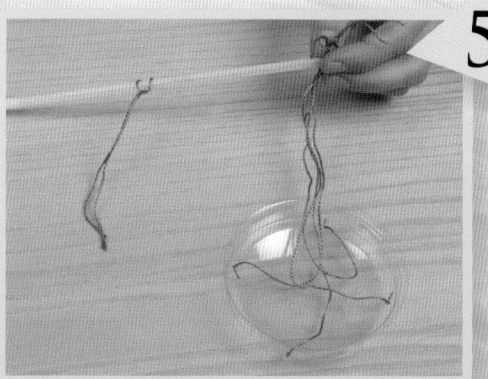

Pull string taut through straw and tie the end to the other lid's strings. Add a string handle and fix with sticky tape.

Hold the scales by the string handle and try balancing small objects in your scales!

CLOTHES AND JEWELLERY

The Vikings needed layers of warm clothing to protect them from winter weather and on long, cold sea voyages. They also wanted their clothes to look good. They enjoyed wearing embroidered cloth and heavy, metal jewellery to display their wealth and their **rank** in society.

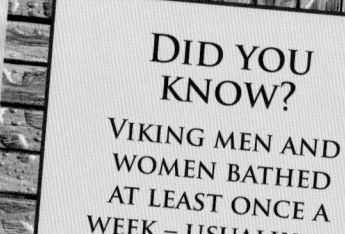

Solid gold brooch (left), made for a very rich Viking leader and a heavy silver arm-ring, worn by a Viking warrior.

FABRIC AND FIBRE

Rich Vikings wore fine wool cloth, dyed in bright colours, or smooth silk and linen. They lined their clothes with fur and trimmed them with braid or embroidery. Poor people wore rough cloth, made from homespun wool or thick, hard-wearing linen. Viking craftswomen also spun and wove fibre from stinging nettles, which produced a soft, silky material.

This rich Viking man is wearing a cosy fur hat, a thick wool cloak and boots of fur-lined leather.

DID YOU KNOW?

VIKING MEN AND WOMEN BATHED AT LEAST ONCE A WEEK – USUALLY ON A SATURDAY – BY HAVING A SAUNA (A BATH IN CLOUDS OF STEAM). THIS AMAZED THE ENGLISH, WHO WASHED LESS OFTEN.

THE VIKING LOOK

Men wore a knee-length tunic, belted round the waist, over an under-shirt and baggy trousers. In cold weather, they added a thick cloak and a hat. Women wore a long under-dress with a pinafore-dress on top, held in place by brooches. In cold weather, they wrapped a big shawl round their shoulders. Married women usually wore a hood-like cap, over long hair tied up in a bun. Viking men, as well as women, wore eye-liner to draw attention to their eyes.

DYE MATERIAL THE VIKING WAY

Vikings used berries and vegetables to dye material beautiful colours. Their dyeing technique still works 1000 years later!

YOU WILL NEED:
1kg RAW BEETROOT • KNIFE • CHOPPING BOARD • RUBBER GLOVES • SAUCEPAN • 1m WHITE COTTON TAPE • WHITE COTTON T-SHIRT • WOODEN SPOON • SIEVE • ACRYLIC PAINT AND BRUSHES • DOUBLE-SIDED STICKY TAPE

1 Chop the beetroot and put it in a saucepan half-filled with cold water. Remember to wear rubber gloves.

2 Put in the tape and T-shirt. Ask an adult to bring it to the boil. Simmer for 1 hour, stirring occasionally.

3 When cool, strain through a sieve. Then remove the tape and T-shirt from the beetroot pulp.

4 Rinse well and hang up to drip dry. Once the tape's dry, paint a Viking pattern along it.

5 When the T-shirt and tape are dry, stick or sew the tape to the T-shirt.

Feel like a proud Viking, in your bright, patterned top. (Don't forget that your top is not colour-fast and should always be washed separately.) ▶

19

FOOD AND DRINK

Vikings ate two meals a day: early in the morning, and in the evening after the day's work was done. Usually, food was simple, but Vikings loved feasting on special occasions, such as Yule (the midwinter festival) or weddings.

Norman warriors feasting. You can see knives and platters on the table and two men holding drinking bowls (left).

FINE FARE
Meals were based on grains. Oats were boiled to make porridge while barley and rye were ground into flour, mixed with water, and baked as 'flat bread'. Vikings also liked meat and fish, stewed or spit-roasted. They made butter and cheese from milk, sausages from blood, and spicy relishes from mustard and garlic. In winter, Vikings ate thick vegetable stews, and warming soup made from dried peas. In summer, they loved to eat fresh fruit and wild woodland berries. They drank water, milk or ale brewed from barley.

USEFUL UTENSILS
Vikings ate from wooden platters or soapstone bowls. They cut and speared food with knives, or sipped from spoons carved from wood or sheep's horn. Poor people drank from wooden mugs or bowls. Rich people used glass or silver cups, or huge drinking horns. Viking women did the cooking, and preserved food to eat in the winter. They salted fish and meat, smoked them above cooking fires, and used ice, for deep-freezing.

Vikings made huge cups for drinking from animal horn. They could not be put down without spilling the contents, so they were only used at feasts and other special occasions.

Drink Viking Apple Juice

Warm, sweet apple juice wasn't only tasty, it kept out the cold! Make some, with a little help from an adult, and sup like a Viking!

YOU WILL NEED:
2 APPLES • KNIFE • 500ml WATER • 1tsp CLEAR HONEY • SAUCEPAN • SIEVE • WOODEN SPOON • HEATPROOF JUG • MUG

1 Wash the apples. Ask an adult to remove the pips and cores, and chop the rest into thin slices.

2 Put the apple slices, cold water and a teaspoon of clear honey into a saucepan.

3 Ask an adult to heat the mixture, stirring well until it starts to boil. Then remove from the heat.

Before you drink, wish your friends 'Good Health!', just like a Viking would have done.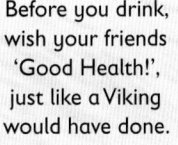

4 Ask an adult to strain the mixture into a jug. Once it's cooled a little, pour some into a mug and drink!

Sports, Games and Music

The Vikings loved sport, board games and story-telling. Playing sport was a good way to show off strength, fitness and skill. Many sports were also excellent training for war. Viking summer games included swimming, wrestling, running, jumping, skating and weightlifting. In winter, Viking men and boys played games rather like ice hockey on frozen rivers and lakes. Vikings played to win, and competitors were often injured. They also liked to watch violent fights between animals, especially horses.

Viking wrestlers fought fiercely. The loser might end up badly hurt.

Play Hnef-tafl

Hnef-tafl (say Neff-tah-fell) means 'king's table'. One player must protect the king from his opponent's much larger army!

YOU WILL NEED:
CORRUGATED CARD • PENCIL • RULER • RED AND BLACK FELT-TIP PENS • AIR-DRYING CLAY • MODELLING TOOL • 24 CHUNKY BLUE BEADS • 12 CHUNKY WHITE BEADS

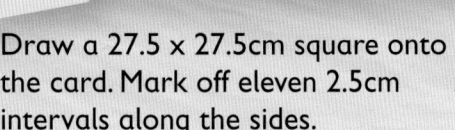

1

Draw a 27.5 x 27.5cm square onto the card. Mark off eleven 2.5cm intervals along the sides.

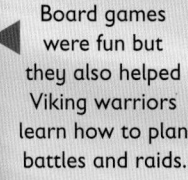

Board games were fun but they also helped Viking warriors learn how to plan battles and raids.

3

Design some Viking-style patterns on spare paper. Draw your best design onto each of the red squares.

INDOOR GAMES

Peaceful pastimes included board games, dice and knucklebones (played like 'jacks' today). Children played with toy boats, model horses, dolls, spinning tops and wooden weapons. Dancing, acrobatics and juggling – sometimes using knives! – were popular among Viking warriors.

AROUND THE FIRE

At feasts, and on long, dark, winter evenings, Viking families and their guests liked to sit round the fire, listening to music and story-telling. Songs and dances were played on harps, **lyres**, whistles and drums. Kings and chiefs paid poets to compose special songs that praised them. Professional entertainers travelled from village to village, **reciting** poems and telling stories.

2

Join up your marks to make a grid. Colour in the four corner squares and the square in the centre.

4

To make the king, shape a 2cm high cylinder from clay. Use a modelling tool to draw on his face and beard.

DID YOU KNOW?

VIKINGS WERE FOND OF RIDDLES AND PROVERBS (WISE SAYINGS) SUCH AS 'GENEROUS AND BRAVE MEN GET THE BEST OUT OF LIFE'.

Set up your board like this before you start each game.
▼

HOW TO PLAY

RULES FOR TWO PLAYERS

The white army's aim is to get the king safely to any of the four corners. The blue army's aim is to capture the king. The game is over when one army achieves its aim. You can move each piece horizontally or vertically as many squares as you wish but you must land on an empty square. Only the king can stop on the red squares. To capture an enemy counter, sandwich it between two of your pieces (see below) or between your piece and a corner square. You can take more than one piece in a go. The blue army starts!

EXAMPLE

If the black piece lands here, both white pieces have black pieces on either side. So, the white pieces are trapped and can be taken.

GODS AND HEROES

The Vikings **worshipped** many different gods and goddesses. Odin was the god of war. The Vikings believed that he could see into the future and was wise, cruel and mysterious. Kings and warriors asked him for protection. Thor, the thunder god, was strong but stupid. He fought giants, ruled the weather and protected farmers. Frey, and his sister, Freya (say Fray-yah), were generous and life-giving. Valkyries (say Val-keer-eez) were sky-goddesses, who flew high above battles. They collected the spirits of men who had died bravely and carried them off to warrior heaven called Valhalla (say Val-hal-lah).

◀ Little metal statue of the goddess Freya. Vikings said she made people, animals and plants grow strong and healthy.

DID YOU KNOW?

SOME DAYS OF THE WEEK ARE STILL NAMED AFTER VIKING GODS, SUCH AS 'THURSDAY' WHICH MEANS 'THOR'S DAY'.

SPIRITS, MONSTERS AND STORIES

Vikings believed in elves, giants, **trolls** and other nature spirits. They loved stories about gods, monsters, heroes and adventures. Many stories told how the whole world – including the gods – was destined to be destroyed at Ragnarok (say Rag-narr-ok), a terrible final battle.

PLEASING THE GODS

Belief in gods helped Vikings cope with their tough, difficult lives. They prayed to gods before going into battle or setting off on long journeys. They offered them food and drink, to ask for favours. In wooden temples, they offered the gods animal **sacrifices**.

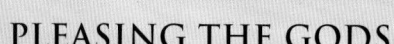

▲ Viking men and women liked to carry amulets (lucky charms). Many were shaped like the magic hammer used by the god Thor when he fought giants and monsters.

Mould Thor's Hammer

Viking blacksmiths poured molten metal into moulds to make objects in special shapes. You can do the same with plaster of Paris!

YOU WILL NEED:
NON-DRYING CLAY • RULER • MODELLING TOOLS • OLD PEN TOP • PLASTER OF PARIS MIXTURE (ALWAYS FOLLOW THE INSTRUCTIONS ON THE PACKET)

1 Shape non-drying clay into a small block. Press the sides against a ruler to make them smooth and straight.

2 With a modelling tool, scoop out the hammer shape. Be careful not to go through the bottom!

3 Press a pen top into the bottom of your mould to make circle patterns on your hammer.

4 Following the instructions on the packet, mix up the plaster of Paris. Pour it up to the top of the mould.

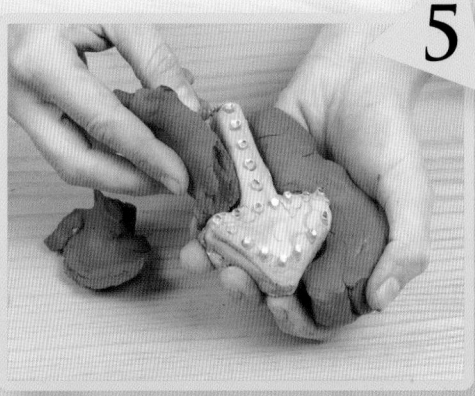

5 When the plaster of Paris has completely dried, carefully peel away the clay mould to reveal your amulet.

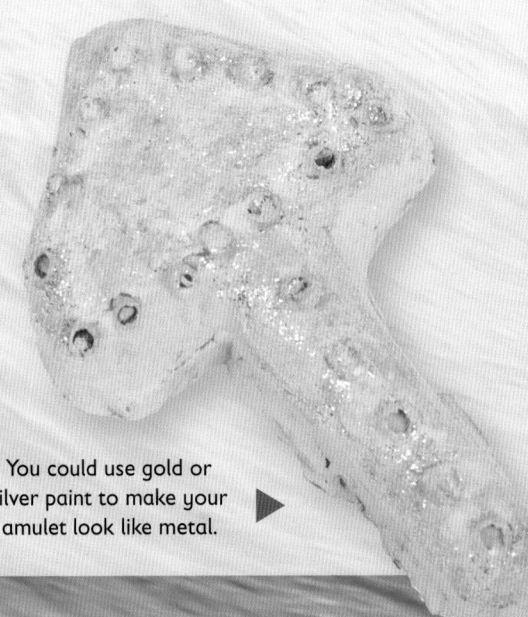

You could use gold or silver paint to make your amulet look like metal. ▶

BURIED TREASURES

The Vikings thought that when a person died, their spirit lived on. Warriors and unmarried girls went to live with Odin and Freya in the sky. Old or sick people went to a cold kingdom ruled by Hel, a gloomy, scary goddess. Ordinary peoples' spirits stayed close to their graves – and sometimes haunted the living.

READY FOR THE NEXT LIFE

In early Viking times, dead bodies were burned. Vikings thought the fires set dead peoples' spirits free from their bodies. Before burning, dead people were given everything they might need in the next world, such as clothes, weapons, jewellery and food. Sometimes slaves were killed, to serve their owners after death. After burning, dead peoples' ashes were scattered or buried in pottery jars.

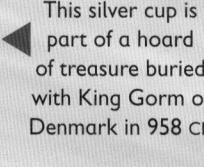

The ashes or bodies of dead Vikings were sometimes surrounded by ship-shaped arrangements of stones.

This silver cup is part of a hoard of treasure buried with King Gorm of Denmark in 958 CE.

DID YOU KNOW?

VIKINGS BURIED TREASURE TO KEEP IT SAFE BUT THEY OFTEN DIED OR WERE KILLED BEFORE THEY COULD DIG IT UP AGAIN. MANY OF THESE HOARDS HAVE BEEN FOUND LONG AFTER VIKING TIMES.

MESSAGES FROM THE PAST

After around 850 CE, most Viking dead bodies were not burned. Important people were buried in real ships, or ship-shaped wooden coffins. Everyone else was buried in holes in the ground. Many of the objects buried in these graves have survived until today. **Archaeologists** have discovered a lot about Viking ideas, designs and skills from grave goods.

MAKE GORM'S CUP

Make a Viking King's silver cup. Imagine being a Viking silversmith as you create patterns by pressing down into the foil.

1

Cut out three foil rectangles that will fit round your cup. Use double-sided sticky tape to stick them together.

2

Copy the design on page 26 onto tracing paper. Put it on the foil. With a blunt pencil, press over each line.

3

Rub black poster paint over the foil. Now gently wipe it away with clean cotton wool.

4

Trim the plastic cup down so that it's slightly shorter than the height of your foil drawing.

5

Wrap the foil around the cup and fix at the back with sticky tape. Fold excess foil in around the rim.

You can't drink from Gorm's cup but you could keep pens and pencils in it. ▶

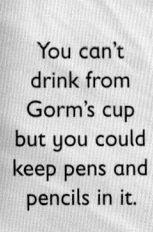

PICTURE STONES AND RUNES

The Vikings used an ancient system of writing, called runes. Each letter was made of straight and diagonal lines because these were easier to carve into stone or wood than curves. Over 2500 Viking **inscriptions** in runes have survived. Some are labels, to show who owned an object. Some are letters or messages. Some are magic spells. Many of the finest are carved on tall stones. These were put up by families to remember people who had died, or by proud individuals who wanted to boast about their own achievements. Some stones only have runic writing while others are carved with pictures from Viking myths and legends.

◀ A Viking picture stone. It has pictures of two snakes (top) and two dragons, with writing in runes around the outer edge.

▲ A Viking carved the runic alphabet into this piece of pine. It also has magical messages carved on the back.

WRITE YOUR NAME IN RUNES

Find out what your name looks like in runes and then write it into soft balsa wood or card. Why not make one as a present for a friend, too?

YOU WILL NEED:
PIECE OF BALSA WOOD OR THICK CARD • PENCIL • PAPER • BLACK FELT-TIP PEN • WOOL • STICKY TAPE

1

Using the chart opposite, find and write down the runes that stand for the letters of your name.

OLD, OLD STORIES

Historians do not know how many Viking people could read and write runes. Stories were passed on by word of mouth from older to younger people, and safely remembered for hundreds of years. Long after Viking times, scholars began to write down all the old Viking histories, adventures and poems. They called Viking stories 'sagas' (say sah-gaz) and their poems 'eddas' (say edd-ahz).

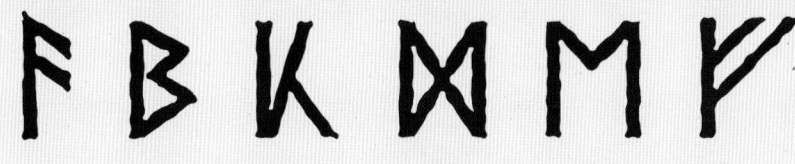

A   B   C   D   E   F

G   H   I   J   K   L   M

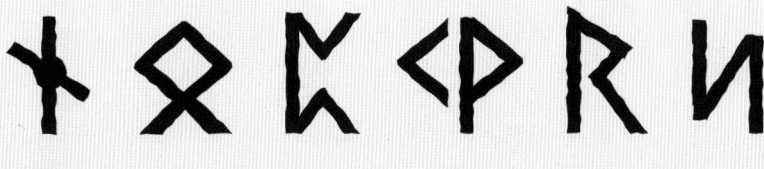

N   O   P   Q   R   S

T   U   V   W   X   Y   Z

DID YOU KNOW?

IMPORTANT PEOPLE PAID POETS CALLED SKALDS (SAY SKALLDZZ) TO SING POEMS PRAISING THEMSELVES AND THEIR GUESTS.

◀ Hang your Viking name sign on your bedroom door.

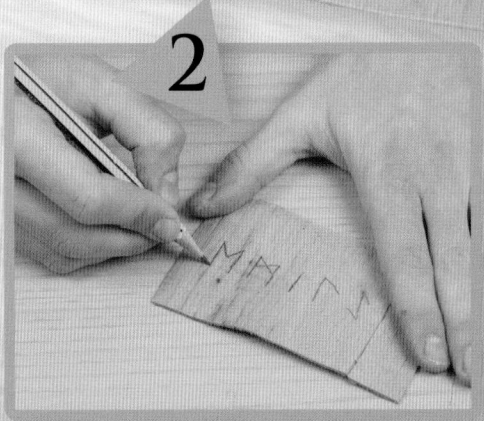

Draw each rune onto the balsa wood or card. Use a pencil and press hard as you draw.

With a felt-tip pen, go over each of your runes. Then attach a loop of wool to the back with sticky tape.

29

GLOSSARY

archaeologist Someone who studies the past by digging up ancient objects or bones.

barter To exchange goods for others of equal value.

Bayeux Tapestry A 70 metre-long embroidered cloth showing the battle of Hastings, which took place in England, in 1066 CE.

close quarters Very near.

hull The hollow, lower part of a ship.

inscription Writing carved into wood or stone.

jarl A Viking nobleman and war-leader.

keel A long, strong piece of wood that acts like a backbone in a ship's hull.

lyre A musical instrument with strings, like a small harp.

mast A tall pole that holds up a ship's sails.

merchant Trader.

Norman A Viking whose family had settled in northern France.

prow The front end of a ship.

rank A person's place in society.

reciting Repeating from memory.

sacrifice A person or animal who is killed to please the gods.

settler Person who leaves their home to live in a new land.

stern Back end of a ship.

troll Small, cruel, cunning Viking monster with a long beard. Vikings said that trolls attacked travellers.

tunic Long, straight piece of clothing with no sleeves.

worship To respect and love a god or goddess.

INDEX

NOTES FOR PARENTS AND TEACHERS

• Research Viking myths and legends about the creation of the world, from library books or a website such as http://www.cdli.ca/CITE/v_creation. htm. Discuss the story with the children, and then help them to plan and make a picture book, retelling the creation myth. This could be a group project, with each child responsible for a different episode in the story.

• Viking musicians played lyres (harps), handbells, animal-horn trumpets and whistles made of bone, accompanied by wooden clappers or hand-clapping. Listen to an ancient Viking song 'Drømde mig en drøm' ('I dreamed a dream last night') played on a lyre at http://www.vikinganswerlady.com/music. shtml#Reconstruction. Help the children to learn to play this tune, and to write their own songs on a dream theme.

• The Vikings loved nicknames. These were often funny, but could also be very revealing about an individual's appearance or character. Ask the children to invent nicknames they'd like to have for themselves, or to draw cartoon characters illustrating some real Viking nicknames. You can find a list at http://www.regia.org/members/names.htm#VikF

• With the children, find out more about Viking ships and make a big map to show where the Vikings sailed. You could decorate the map with cut-outs of different Viking ships, sea-creatures and sea monsters like the famous Kraken (giant squid). For pictures of Viking ships, see http://www.khm.uio. no/english/viking_ship_museum/ and http://www.copenhagenpictures.dk/vik_skib.html. For a virtual Viking voyage online, and much more, see: http://www.mnh.si.edu/vikings/start.html.

• Simple Viking jewellery is fun and easy to make. The children could string coloured glass beads on a cord to make a Viking-style necklace (see, for example, http://www.gov.im/mnh/collections/archaeology/vikings/paganlady.xml). Or they could trace wavy Viking patterns from a book onto a strip of card or leather to make a Viking wristband.

Useful websites
Try this helpful site, with information, quizzes and activities, supported by the Norwegian Ministry of Education: http://www.viking.no/. It welcomes visitors with a charming Viking 'greeting' poem, which would be easy for most children to learn.

Simple information for children, and a great many links (some for adults, some for children) can be found at http://worldhistory.mrdonn.org/vikings.html.

To see a list of Viking reenactment groups visit http://www.clash-of-steel.co.uk/pages/links_groups.php?cat=Viking